Happiness is The Truth

A Book of God's Love, Hope and Inspiration

Michael John DeNucci

Michael John DeNucci

Cumberland, WI

Second Edition

November, 2023

Printed in the United States

By http://thebookpatch.com

ISBN: 9798890902627

First Edition December, 2021

Acknowledgments

First and foremost, I thank God who, through the Holy Spirit, inspired me to write this book. My gratitude to God is overwhelming!

Also, I thank my brother Donald for support in writing this book and for facilitating its printing.

Table of Contents

Preface

God is Love. Love is the Truth.
God is Happiness. Therefore,
Happiness is the Truth.

Introduction

1
Enjoying the Moment

At times we get so caught up in our plans for the future that we forget to enjoy the present—enjoy the moment. That moment will never be ours again—it will slip away into the past and probably be forgotten.

Like the song "Today" sung by the New Christy Minstrels and written by Randy Sparks, "I can't be contented with yesterday's glory and I can't live on promises winter to spring. Today is my moment and now is my story...."

Jesus said not to worry about tomorrow. Look to the birds and the lilies—do not worry about what you will eat or wear—how we will nourish ourselves and dress. Enjoy the day—the moment.

2
Are We Either Good or Bad?

We are not simply either good or bad. No, we are all sinners, so we are all "bad" sometimes and "good" probably much of the time. We need to remember to be humble to be "good" rather than being too proud, which can lead us to sin.

3
The Damage of Ignorance versus the Truth

Ignorance comes with a price. False beliefs from ignorance or superstition damage us.

Someone once told me that when she was a child, somebody told her that left-handedness indicated mental retardation. Since she was left-handed, that false accusation hurt her in her childhood and even later in her adult life.

Think of whether Christopher Columbus would have discovered the New World, if he had continued with the earlier belief that the world was "flat".

Also, in Scripture, Jesus was asked: what sin had his parents committed to cause their son to suffer an "affliction?". Jesus answered: this condition was not caused by anyone's sin, but to show God's power to cure the affliction, which Jesus did.

Our search for the truth must continue, not only in spiritual and philosophical matters, but also in science to erase ignorance. Scripture says: know the truth and it will set you free.

4
True Happiness

The song "True, True Happiness" sung by Johnny Tillotson and written by Hal Greene and Richard Wolf said, "true, true happiness will follow if you only follow me." Jesus said "come follow me" with that same promise.

5
Love: More Important than Agreement

Jesus said to his apostles just before leaving them with His Ascension into Heaven: "Love one another as I love you". Scripture also says that His followers will be known by the way they "love one another".

Notice it does NOT say they will be known how they "agree with each other", but how they "love one another." Love is more important than agreement. It requires that we go beyond our disagreements to find unity through love. This principle is important in all human relationships, including politics. Let's love one another despite our differences of opinions and beliefs.

6
Does God Rejoice when We Express Love to Him?

An interesting concept to me is that God rejoices when we express love to Him either in prayer, good deeds or repentance from sin.

God is a living Being and we were created in His image and likeness. Like us, it seems that He would rejoice when receiving love.

The parable of the "prodigal son" sheds some light on this issue. The son's father rejoiced on learning of his son's return after leaving his father to squander wealth given from him. His father was so elated, that he "slaughtered the fatted calf" and had a celebration to welcome his son back. Perhaps, God rejoices when we come back to Him after repenting of sin, or simply expressing love to Him in prayer or good deeds.

7
Evil and Satan

Jesus referred to the apostle Peter as "Satan" when Peter argued with Jesus about His future passion and death. Jesus said: "Get behind me Satan. You think not as God does, but as humans do." Satan thrives on ignorance and influenced Peter's thinking at that time.

Our selfish desires cause us to sin against God. These desires are often the result of what others have said to us, but it is our decision to sin when we succumb to temptation. Sometimes, we are tempted by the devil or others to sin, but the choice is still ours.

If we turn our minds to God, we are not as likely to succumb to temptation, but, rather, pursue virtue. Love is the greatest virtue—Love of God and Neighbor as Ourselves. Love leads to Happiness, and Happiness is the Truth.

8
Freedom: Choosing God or our Selfish Desires

Some people desire almost unlimited freedom-to choose to do almost whatever they desire. However, this philosophy can lead us to slavery due to sin rather than freedom. Surrender to God to have true freedom and safety under His protection. Happiness is the Truth because it comes from God.

9
Where Has the Respect Gone?

In the last few years our society has seen more civil unrest resulting from a lack of respect among some of us. First, a lack of respect for some Blacks by some police officers. Then, a lack of respect for some police officers by many persons. Then a lack of respect for migrants trying to enter the country without going through the proper channels. Finally, a lack of respect for officials, both elected and unelected, at different levels of government, including some who have had threats on their lives. (Consider the violent attack at our nation's capital in January of 2021.)

Some of us have neglected to respect others who we feel have offended us. It has been said that "violence begets violence". So, it is with disrespect. It spreads like a cancer and threatens to tear apart the fabric of our institutions, including our right to vote, and other democratic values and rights, as well as peace in our society.

Jesus said: "Love your enemies." If we cannot do that, at least respect others if you do view them as the enemy. However, love with respect is the best answer based on the Commandments of Love from Jesus, one of which is: "Love your neighbor as yourself."

Let's bring back Respect based on Love, the Truth and Understanding. Understanding is a gift of the Holy Spirit which can give us the knowledge and strength to respect each other to have a more civilized society and functional government. Love is the means by which we can achieve Happiness, and Happiness is the Truth.

10
Forgiveness

He who forgives much will, in turn, be forgiven much. The Lord's Prayer says: "Forgive us our trespasses as we forgive those who trespass against us." This implies that we must forgive others to be forgiven by God.

The case from scripture of the unforgiving servant comes to mind. The master forgave his servant of his debts. Then, that servant met his own servant who asked for debt forgiveness, but the superior servant refused to do so. Scripture tells us that the head master punished that unforgiving servant. So it is with God, according to that lesson from Scripture. We must forgive others to be forgiven by God.

Finally, those who repent from the most serious sins—who have most need for forgiveness—find more rejoicing in Heaven from their repentance than those with little need of forgiveness. Remember the lesson of the "prodigal son" story in Scripture, which I referred to in article 6 of this book.

11
Isn't God Awesome?

God has pulled me through so many tight spots that I cannot ignore His will and protection in what has happened in my life, whether it be in "close calls" for accidents or simply timing in meeting persons who became important in my life, like my wife Kathy and my friend Kristina Young. God's plan has unfolded, not always in a good way for me, but perhaps, that too was meant to increase my faith in Him. But many times, God has clearly shown me that I am in His protection. The following six stories from my life and the seventh story, from another's experience, describe that protection.

12
First Near Accident

One near accident for me occurred in 1968 in my first car-a 1957 Buick. I was set to go to a fraternity party while a student at the College of St. Thomas in St.

Paul, Mn. The other two couples, my date and I got into the car and I attempted to pull away from the curb to start out. But suddenly my steering wheel spun loosely around and around, disconnected from the steering column. I had no control over the vehicle, so the trip in that car was instantly aborted. Fortunately, this loss of steering did not occur when we were in traffic. Imagine the disaster that could have occurred if the steering went out in traffic instead of being stopped at the curb. To me, this was overwhelming evidence that God was watching over me.

13
Running out of Gas

One less dangerous, but important memory was of my driving that 1957 Buick also in about 1968, when I noticed I was really low on gas. Viewing a gas station, I decided to turn in for gas. However, as I was approaching the station, my car began losing power and all power was gone as I pulled into the gas station literally coasting to the pump completely out of gas. Again, I was shown God's watch over me despite my carelessness by not getting gas sooner.

14
Second Near Accident

I had another near accident in another vehicle could have cost the lives of my cousin, his girlfriend, my girlfriend and me.

We had begun a trip from St. Paul to Gooseberry Falls on the North Shore of Lake Superior at about 6:00 A.M. On the way there and while up their things went well for us. However, we stayed late into the evening before starting the trip back, which was longer because we had to drop off my cousin's girlfriend in St. Cloud. All of us were very tired. I was almost falling asleep and not thinking clearly as I was driving. I thought I saw an exit and slowed way down before starting to shift lanes for the "supposed" exit.

My cousin hollered at me from the back seat, when suddenly I heard a car coming up fast behind us. Then, I heard a subtle, but definite "ting" of our car being grazed by the car coming from behind. It was a very close call. I was so shaken up that I pulled over and asked my cousin to drive, which he did. God's saving grace and protection is still vivid in my mind.

15
·The Accident

In 1970, I was driving in a neighborhood near St. Thomas College about to enter an "unmarked intersection"-no traffic signs or lights-more common back then than today, when I slowed down and checked for traffic. I saw a car far away coming toward the intersection. Being already at the intersection, I proceeded forward through it, feeling "safe." However, just before leaving the intersection that car barreled into my car so fast that he pushed my car around cutting off a regular street sign and severely damaging my car. Fortunately, I was uninjured. I instructed someone to call police. A policeman came and gave ME a ticket for "failure to yield". The other car seemed less seriously damaged, but the driver's passenger in the other car had a bump on her head. Later, I received a bill from the city for the damaged street sign, which I immediately paid. Then, I received a notice of a lawsuit against me from the other driver for $30,000 due to property damage, injury to his passenger and mental anguish.

I felt my life was ruined. $30,000 was like $300,000 in today's money and I had very little money. Also, I had the least liability insurance possible—$10,000-$30,000. I did not believe I was at fault, so I decided to fight the $85.00 ticket in court. I presented the case myself and the case was dismissed, so I won. But I still had the civil suit to tend with. I felt that my winning concerning the ticket would help that case, which I believe it actually did. After describing my version of the accident to my insurance company, I got a letter that the lawsuit was settled out of court for a nominal fee.

Finally, it was unfortunate that the other driver's negligent driving—speeding through an unmarked intersection—caused the injury to the driver's passenger. However, I knew I was not at fault, but still vowed that in the future I would not assume anything about other drivers' actions. God watched over me so that I could move on with my life under His protection. I am still so thankful to God.

16
The Timely Prize

While between jobs and almost out of money, I decided to go ice fishing on Lake Minnetonka west of Minneapolis while living in Minneapolis. My plan was to catch some fish for cheap food. On my way back, after catching no fish, I heard an announcement on the radio station to which I was listening that anyone with a last name on a certain page between beginning letters for those names in the phone book could call in to receive $97.00. I knew my name was on that page, and with no cell phone then in 1974, I pulled into a gas station right after hearing the announcement. Then, I called the radio station on a pay phone at the gas station. Indeed, I did win the prize which was enough to cover the car payment that month! Without the prize, I probably wouldn't have had enough money to cover my car payment. Once again God came through for me with the timing of that activity. He certainly has been important in my life's events through His intercession and protection.

17
The Dangerous Fire

Many years later I was living back in Cumberland and working at the Post Office in Spooner, Wisconsin. One night on the trip to Spooner to work the night shift, I noticed my relatively new car—still under warranty— began losing power about two miles south of Shell Lake. It was in December, so the weather was cold. I was forced to cruise powerless to the shoulder when I noticed smoke and/or steam coming out from under my hood. When I opened the hood, I found a hose on fire. Not knowing what else to do, I simply blew hard on the flame. Much to my surprise the fire went out. Then, I noticed the motor was covered with acorns. Evidently, squirrels had put them there to store for winter.

My car was towed to the dealer where I had bought it, but not covered by warranty for such damage. However, my "comprehensive" feature of my insurance covered the total replacement of the carburetor because the damage was due to animals. So, my $900 bill was fully paid.

But money was not the big issue. What if the gas had

ignited and exploded in my face when looking under the hood? Once again, God kept me safe. I am so grateful to Him for helping me through another dangerous situation.

18
God's Protection in Another's Accident

A recent car accident involved a young man who was seriously hurt by what is thought to be a reckless driver. The young man was hit head-on in his vehicle by the other car, thought to be traveling at a high speed in the young man's lane. After the collision, the young man's car caught on fire, but he was removed from the car, just before the fire, by persons passing by, thus, averting suffering or death from the fire.

The young man, perhaps miraculously, was spared his life, though seriously injured. He is requiring reconstructive surgery after sustaining severe injuries.

However, God showed His protection over that young man by sparing his life with no permanent brain or internal injuries. Truly, God cares and sometimes intervenes to protect those He loves.

19
Is God Fun?

I believe that many people think of God as a tyrant who wants to punish us or a boring, old man with no sense of excitement or humor, and who does not like music. Finally, some people believe that God is aloof and does not care about us. To me, those views of God are very inaccurate and lead to separation from God. At best, such views could cause us to worry about our relationship to Him.

Jesus told us not to worry. I interpret that to mean He does not even want us to worry about Him, but simply to love and trust Him. God knows us better than we know ourselves and He wants to share in our lives—including our excitement, laughter and music.

Scripture says that eye has not seen, ear has not heard and mind has not imagined what God has in store for those who love Him, when referring to Heaven. It would seem to me that, based on that statement, God is exciting and even Fun! God is Love, Happiness and the Truth. Happiness is the Truth!

20
Does Pride Come from Self-Love?

Pride may be simply feeling good about ourselves because of some achievement we have made. We can enjoy our achievements according to the Desiderata poem. However, we should not let pride become so strong or powerful that we lose an honest image of ourselves. This inflated image of ourselves shows that we lack humility.

This inflated self-image from pride does not come from true self love, because true self love from humility gives us an honest image of ourselves. Excessive self-love is said to be narcissistic, but not really so because it is not our true self we are loving, but some false idea of ourselves. True self love means that we love our "true selves" based on humility. It comes from love of God and facilitates love of our Neighbor as Ourselves.

Furthermore, excessive pride can lead to "snobbery" towards others and even towards God. Practice humility and be careful of pride, which can threaten or destroy our Happiness. God is Love, the Truth and Happiness.

21
Is Humility Low Self-Esteem?

I think that, sometimes, my self-esteem was very low when I had self-doubts about my accomplishments. For example, I questioned my brother about who had named the titles for my articles in my first book: "Thoughts and Writings." He said that I had. This surprised me because I thought he had named them when putting the book together based on my text messages to my siblings. At other times, I thought my books were boing, repetitious or even critical of established religions. However, my siblings expressed support and complimented me on my books.

I must remember that I do believe that the Holy Spirit inspired me to write the books, so I should feel good about myself concerning the books.

Another brother told me on his death bed that I should not "sell myself short." I will never forget those words as his life ended. He must have known that I had low self-esteem at times.

Finally, low self-esteem is not necessarily humility. Humility brings us to see ourselves as we really are, not less than we really are. Thus, humility can work to give us honesty about ourselves. Therein lies Happiness which comes from God, who is the Truth. Therefore, Happiness is the Truth.

22
Separation of Church and State: Freedom of Speech

Our nation was founded on a belief in separation of church and state. However, the Declaration of Independence written by Thomas Jefferson in 1776 states that "We hold these truths to be self-evident, that all men are created equal and that they are endowed by their Creator with certain unalienable rights, that among these are Life, Liberty and the Pursuit of Happiness." Notice that it states that these rights are "endowed by their Creator." It would seem that "Creator" refers to "'God." If so, it says that God Himself grants us the right to the "Pursuit of Happiness."

Also, our Pledge of Allegiance refers to "one nation under God." The phrase "under God" was added in 1954 under President Eisenhower at the urging of the Catholic Knights of Columbus and Veteran organizations. Also, the inscription on the outside wall of the local American Legion is "For God and Country." In a meeting I attended at the local American Legion, a prayer was said at the meeting.

The principle that the state is not to establish a religion was laid out by our founding fathers to maintain freedom of religion, since some of those founders escaped a denial of such freedom in their homeland of England.

However, to deny the people the "right' to express their religious beliefs—even in public—is, to me, denying freedom of speech.

We should not let ourselves be so afraid of "talking about religion" that we become an atheistic society much like Communist societies were and, perhaps, still are today to some degree. We are guaranteed freedom of speech by the First Amendment:

"Congress shall make no law respecting establishment of religion, or prohibiting free exercise Thereof; or Abridging the Freedom of Speech..."

Thus, we still have a Constitutional right to express religion in public, which can promote our "Pursuit of Happiness", which comes from God, who is Happiness and the Truth.

23
Suffering from Disasters and Wars: God and Free Will

Some, if not many, people believe that God doesn't care about people because He allows so many natural disasters and man-made disasters (wars) that cause so much suffering for mankind.

Natural disasters, even diseases, are considered to be

an "Act of God." So, some people blame God for those disasters. However, God tests people through the laws of nature including earthquakes, hurricanes, floods, tornadoes, etc. Such disasters can bring us closer to God out of need and these disasters can bring us closer to each other when people try to alleviate the suffering caused by the disasters. Consider Job in the Old Testament. He lost much of his wealth and even his loved ones, but God heard his complaining and gave him more wealth than he had before his calamities. Thus, Job's faith in God carried him through the calamities he had endured. This can be an effect of disasters with mankind today.

Even diseases, such as Covid 19, I believe, have brought people to consider the issue of priorities in life. Often, these priorities can become or remain God and significant others (family, friends). And God did not forsake us when Covid hit. Instead, He inspired the researchers to rapidly develop a vaccine to greatly mitigate the spread of the disease. God cares.

Concerning wars, it is important to remember that mankind has "free will," which includes the freedom to wage war, even with all its terrible consequences. However, I believe Good eventually wins over evil, even in war. Consider World War Two. I believe that we won that war because God was "with us." God always wins because He is the Truth and Happiness is the Truth.

24
What is Meditation?

Meditation is NOT putting oneself into some sort of "trance." When I first read about meditation, it was directed that I free my mind of all thoughts and concentrate on their word "I". I found it very difficult to do that.

Now, after looking to the dictionary meaning of meditation, I find it is simply contemplation: reflecting upon a subject. To me that subject is not "I", but "God." I believe we can meditate on important issues by simply "thinking" about them in a "free flowing fashion"—not forcing our thoughts.

Meditation is relaxing, and physically and mentally restorative for me. The benefits of meditation—relaxation, etc., —have been reported and proposed. It is a valid "activity." Notice that I say "activity." It is not being "idle." I use meditation to write my books. It does have value, especially when the focus is on God, which is the main topic of my books.

Use meditation to free our minds of worry by focusing on the value of God in our lives to bring us Happiness, which is the Truth, because it comes from God, who is the Truth.

25
Does Purgatory Exist

The Catholic Church began and maintained the belief in purgatory defined as temporary suffering (i.e., the fires of hell) due to venial sins or penance due to mortal sins already forgiven while living on earth. I did not find Jesus speaking of purgatory in Scripture.

To me, the idea of physical suffering in some temporary hell is dubious, at best. I cannot believe that God would be so cruel as to burn us in some "hellfire" before entering heaven. Even hell I have described, not as a place of physical torment, but as an alienation from God—a condition of hopelessness—which would be terrible enough.

However, I do believe that some of us, after we die are not ready for heaven and need to undergo a temporary state of refinement or education to prepare us for heaven so that we can "fit in there." To me, this temporary state of "refinement" or "education" defines purgatory. A religious sister once explained her version of purgatory that way. Also, I do not believe in any physical suffering for sins already forgiven while on earth, even mortal sins.

Happiness is the Truth because it is what God desires for all of us. It is our decision whether to accept or reject that Happiness, which results in the condition of our soul at end of this lifetime.

26
Purgatory: Does it Lead to Fearing Death?

The idea of Purgatory can be a source of pain and fear for us rather than hope for a transition into heaven. Why would anyone look forward to a happy death when it could mean "temporary hell" with all the physical suffering from the "fires of hell"? Why could not that belief cause us to fear death?

I propose that we do not fear death or purgatory, because both may be necessary for our entry into heaven—our true hope. Do not fear purgatory, but view it as a "refinement" to prepare us for heaven, with no physical suffering.

We pray for a happy death. While "fearing" purgatory, it is difficult for me to envision a happy death. Look to immediate acceptance into heaven after we die, but accept a temporary refinement in purgatory, if needed, to prepare us for heaven. If we pray for a happy death, I believe God will grant that wish because He desires Happiness for all of us.

27
Analyzing Happiness

I just woke up from a nap to a love song before writing this article. I started to think that I was happy and tried to analyze why I was happy. Perhaps, I was refreshed by my nap or enjoyed the love song or both. Anyway, I realize that it can be difficult sometimes to know why we feel happy. I am never completely satisfied with the reason for my happiness.

We may never get a final answer by attempting to analyze why we are happy. Perhaps, we should simply accept it as a gift from God because He loves us. Happiness is the truth because it is a free gift from God.

28
Spiritual Assets: Gift and Fruits of the Holy Spirit

The Fruits of the Holy Spirit are: Charity, Joy, Peace, Patience, Kindness, Goodness, Generosity, Gentleness, Faithfulness, Modesty, Self-Control and Chastity.

The Gifts of the Holy Spirit are: Wisdom, Understanding, Knowledge, Counsel, Piety, Fortitude and Fear of the Lord.

The world needs these spiritual assets to find and promote Peace and Happiness, which comes from God through these Fruits and Gifts of the Holy Spirit.

29
Anticipation of Heaven: A Source of Happiness

If we believe in Christ's promise of everlasting life—everlasting happiness—that belief can bring us happiness in this lifetime. Consider an atheist's belief in no afterlife or a person who believes there is a God, but that the afterlife means a lot of suffering and torment. Compare those beliefs to a follower of Christ keeping His commandments of Love and looking forward to eternal bliss after leaving this world. That anticipation of Heaven can bring us Happiness in this lifetime.

30
By The Rivers of Babylon

"Let the words of our mouths and the meditation of our hearts be acceptable in thy sight here tonight.... carry us away in captivity requiring of us a song. Now, how should we sing the Lord's song in a strange land? By the rivers of Babylon where we sat down, we wept when we remembered Zion." (Jerusalem).

The above quote is from the song By the Rivers of Babylon sung by the group Boney M and written and recorded by Brent Dowe and Trevor McNaughton, Frank Farian and Reyam. It is produced by Frank Farian. The lesson for the early Jews or Chosen People was that despite captivity in Babylon as punishment for disobeying God, those people prayed that they would be freed and allowed to return to the promised land, which they eventually were.

"The exiles were brought up from Babylon to Jerusalem." Ezra 1, 1:1-4, 11

The lesson in this story for us is that we will suffer if we sin against God, but can be forgiven and redeemed if we repent and pray. God is the source of all love and forgiveness.

31
What is Love?

To me Love is proven when we are available for someone and offer our help when needed. Words can be "cheap" and "actions speak louder than words." However, words can sometimes help someone in need, which can also exemplify Love and lead to Happiness.

32
Live for Today

A song from 1967 sung by the Grassroots and written by Michael Julien, Mogel and David Shapiro, produced by P.F. Sloan and Steve Barri says "Live for today and don't worry about tomorrow." They explain that some people are "in a hurry to complicate their minds by chasing after money and dreams that cannot come true". This is in line within Christ's message not to worry about tomorrow, but be concerned with the present day.

This does not mean we cannot make plans for the future, but we should not "worry" about the future and realize that all plans do not materialize, because so much is "out of our hands." Simply, trust God with our future. He has the final say in that matter.

33
Selling God Short

On his deathbed, my brother said to me: "Don't sell yourself short". I now extend that statement to our attitude towards God. "Don't sell God short."

God is more loving and forgiving than many of us could imagine. Even the worst sinner can be saved, "for all is possible with God." Consider St. Paul who had "persecuted" the early Christians and watched approvingly as St. Stephen became the first Christian martyr. St Paul was known as Saul when struck blind on the road to Damascus. Then, Saul heard Jesus say to him after Christ was crucified: "Saul, Saul why do you persecute me? This marked the beginning of Saul's conversion. After regaining his sight, he became a bold advocate for Jesus, eventually dying for Him as a martyr. His name was changed to Paul after his conversion to become a great Saint.

One should always realize that we are not necessarily worthy of God's forgiveness, but He offers it to us unconditionally because that is His Supernatural quality. God is Love and Happiness.

34
Did Jesus Die as Human Sacrifice to His Father?

No! I do not believe that Jesus Christ died as a human sacrifice to His Father as atonement for sin. To me, the Old Testament belief in sacrifice of a formerly living thing has expired! His death fit the idea of a formerly living sacrifice to God at that time, but I do not believe that God wanted His Son to suffer and die as atonement for sin because that is not in the Supernatural quality of God to do so. God is Love!

Jesus was allowed to die by His Father to give us an example of Love based on the Truth. Jesus said, when questioned by Pontius Pilate, just before His passion and death: "I came to testify to the Truth", which He received from His Father. He did not die as atonement for sins, certainly not our sins, for we were not even living then. We, today, are not responsible for Christ's death, but He died so that we may know the Truth. Jesus Christ actually was the most important martyr for the Truth. The most important Truth to which He testified was the Promise of Everlasting Life if we keep His Commandments of Love of God and Neighbor as Ourselves. He offered and still offers Everlasting Happiness.

None of this is to say that Jesus is not offended when we sin, but that He is offended by sin which we commit sin in our current lifetimes. However, Love is more important than any physical sacrifice one could make to God. Finally, Jesus Christ's Resurrection shows His victory over death and proves that He was and is the Truth, because He had predicted His death and Resurrection.

35
What is Retirement?

Retirement has various meanings, even in the dictionary, which defines it as "to withdraw oneself from business, public life or active service." Another definition is "a secluded place, a retreat."

I truly have enjoyed my "retirement" with more time for fishing and travel, etc. However, I no longer consider myself as "retired," since, as noted at the end of my last books, I am now a "freelance writer for God and mankind." "Freelance" means that I am not tied to any organization. So I am free to write almost whatever I want, almost whenever I want. However, I consider this "work" to be guided by the Holy Spirit, so I write according to that guidance.

Finally, volunteer work done after retiring from "monetarily paid work" is not considered to interrupt or end retirement. Until now I have written my books with no monetary gain, but I have considered myself as working, not really retired. So the common definition of retirement is not correct to me. Even "unpaid work" should be considered work, so one is not really fully "retired" if one does even only that type of work. If such work leads to more Happiness for Others and expresses Love to God, it can bring the "worker" much Happiness.

36
Reciprocated Love from God

Sometimes when we love someone, they do not return or reciprocate the love back to us. However, when we offer our love to God, it is always reciprocated. In fact, God loves us even when we don't love Him. His Love is unconditional and 100% reliable, for God is Love. To know God is to know Love, for God is the source of all Love, Happiness, and Truth because God is Love, Happiness and Truth.

37
Love: Is it Happiness?

I believe that Love is the greatest stimulant or catalyst for Happiness known to man. Love results in Happiness, and It is no coincidence that Love is the CORE teaching of Jesus Christ.

Love is a positive force in society with so many good

side effects or results. It can be helping others with actions, monetary contributions, material gifts or simply kind words and prayer. Love is Truth and Happiness because it originates with God, who is Truth and Happiness.

38
Can God Fit into Our Lives?

I believe that God knows us better than we know ourselves. He knows our joys and fears. God wants us to share our lives with Him—both good and bad times.

He CAN fit into all of our lives, because He knows us so well and wants us to know Him so that We can share all our trials, tribulations and joys with Him. We should remember to share our life experiences with God. He is always there for us and wants us to be happy.

39
Does God Love Music?

Yes! I emphatically believe that God loves music.
Consider all the music in the Christian Churches—all
types of songs with the message of love and praise to
God and, often, love among people. Even the angels in
Heaven are said to sing. ("Hark the Herald Angels
Sing" at Christmas time). Finally, if God loves music in
the Churches, wouldn't He also love songs in the
society at large. Love is Christ's core teaching.
Certainly, songs with that message are loved and
enjoyed by God, just as we love and enjoy such songs.
Happiness is the Truth and music helps us attain and
maintain that Happiness.

40
Appreciating God's Gift: Happiness

When enjoying ecstasy leading to Happiness or simply contentment giving us Happiness, we should enjoy it and not feel guilty as though we do not deserve it. Indeed, if God grants us Happiness, it is His gift to us. It would be rude for us not to humbly accept it and thank Him for it. Happiness is the Truth because it comes from God!

41
Fear Strikes Out

Reminiscent of a TV show many years ago, the title of this article indicates that fear can cause failure in life, as in "striking out" in baseball. If we succumb to fear instead of practicing courage to do something virtuous, which entails some risk, we may "strike out' or fail to achieve some worthy goal. Love is the best motivator, not fear, for God is Love and Happiness—the Truth!

42
Why Do Some of Us Have Trouble Finding Happiness?

Why don't some of us find Happiness at times? Like the song "Looking for Love" sung by Johnny Lee and written by Patti Ryan, Wanda Mellette and Bob Morrison when referring to looking for love, perhaps we are looking for Happiness in the wrong places. Do we look for Happiness totally in other persons, material goods or money?

We should not look completely to others for our Happiness. I have said that only God's love is 100% reliable. People can be fickle. Don't put all your "eggs in the baskets of others," but only in God's basket.

Likewise, do not put "all your eggs" in the basket of material goods or money. Material goods and money can be taken away and, at best, provide only temporary elation or contentment.

Only God can complete us, for only He is Happiness and the Truth!

43
Is God Offended When We Don't Return His Love?

I believe God always loves us, even when we sin and turn away from Him. However, He is offended when we do not return His Love, just as a trusted friend would be offended. But God always forgives us, just as a good friend would do. God can be our best friend if we let Him, for God is Love, Happiness and the Truth!

44
Life Satisfaction

The following is an excerpt from my book "Fishing for Heaven" to again propose that sometimes we must leave our "comfort zone" to experience "enhanced Happiness" by being creative.

"I learned about job satisfaction in my graduate school studies of Industrial Relations. However, that was a rather narrow meaning of satisfaction. What I propose to consider is "Life Satisfaction."

To assume every day will be the same is to put every day on a plateau with no ups or downs. But if we are fixated on that plateau, it can become a rut.

To gain satisfaction in life, we must leave that plateau or rut, at times, and rise above to do something creative, or at least "outside the box."

It is not necessary to feel uncomfortable to move "outside the box," though that could be a result. However, when "outside the box" we may feel inspired to express ourselves in a meaningful way through harnessing our creativity. That can result in life satisfaction, which can mean the beginning of Heaven before our earthly bodies die. Jesus wants us to be happy in this lifetime and upward into the next lifetime.

Keep "fishing for Heaven." If you let Jesus be your guide, you will catch your trophy—Heaven."

45
Divine Providence

I have said that Divine Providence is the "hand we have been dealt" by God and, if we use it wisely, we will find Happiness. However, Divine Providence does not end with that "hand of cards," but is maintained by God with His guidance in our lives. God continues to offer us help along the way, through Scripture, other religious readings, other persons and prayer.

God does NOT say to us: "There, I gave you this life, now it is totally up to you to make it work. You're on your own." No, He offers us guidance along the way.

It is my intent that my books contribute to that guidance and inspire Happiness in this lifetime to lead us to that place we call "Heaven" after our earthly bodies die. Happiness is the Truth since it comes from God, the source of all Love and Happiness.

God Love and Bless You!

Michael John DeNucci lives in Cumberland, WI and is a freelance writer for God and Mankind.

Michael John DeNucci attended his first two years of high school at Holy Cross Seminary in Lacrosse, Wisconsin and then returned to graduate from Cumberland High School. He went on to earn his Bachelor's Degree in Political Science from the College of St Thomas in St Paul, Minnesota, attended the University of Wisconsin at Madison partially completing an MBA, and then earning a Master's Degree in Industrial Relations from the University of Minnesota. He is an Army Veteran who has served stateside and in Germany. He has held a variety of jobs over his lifetime which have broadened his perspectives on the relationship of God and Mankind.

Other Books by Michael John DeNucci

"Thoughts and Writings"

"God is Love"

"Fishing for Heaven"

"Is God Happiness"

"Is Love the Truth"

"Is God Freedom?"

"God Is the Truth"

"Is Love Freedom"

"Is God Mercy"

"Is God Peace?"